D1496339

Praise for Alissa Quart's Poetry

"Dense, aphoristic, playful..."

—*The New Yorker*

"A keen observer of our culture and a believer in the power of poetry to cut to the heart of issues around us: money, class, gender and the environment."

—NPR

"Quart turns the insecure conditions that shape our lives today into beautiful jagged verse: the poetry of careers replaced by gigs, of workplaces transformed into WeWork, of a country with no promise, ever, of simple safety."

—Barbara Ehrenreich, author of *Nickel and Dimed*

"Every movement, from splicing, to condensation to litany, has an unprecedented intensity, informative politics, surprise and audacious flair."

—Wayne Koestenbaum, author of *Camp Marmalade*

"[Her poems] reveal her keen sociological eye and serve as remarkably apt cultural critiques."

—*Publishers Weekly*

"Quart's laser-sharp phrases...have a way of sticking around in your head long after you turn the final page."

—*Alternet*

"The irony of our predicament . . . is delightfully disclosed not only in the speaker's waggish yet tempered tone, but also in the sheer refinement of [her] free verse."

—*The Boston Review*

Thoughts and Prayers

Andrea,
Thanks for coming and sharing

Alex Gs

Thoughts and Prayers

ALISSA QUART

OR Books
New York • London

Visit our website at www.orbooks.com

All rights information: rights@orbooks.com

First printing 2019

Cataloging-in-Publication data is available from the Library of Congress.
A catalog record for this book is available from the British Library.

paperback ISBN 978-1-68219-216-0
e-book ISBN 978-1-68219-220-7

Typeset by Lapiz Digital Services. Printed by Bookmobile, USA, and CPI, UK.

For Cleo

CONTENTS

"But the past is already here, and you are nursing some private project."
—John Ashbery

I.

SAKHALIN

I.

Sanctuary Island, Sakhalin,
a Russian penal colony.
Anton Chekhov traveled
here by rail, long
months from Moscow,
tubercular. Took
a transcendent census
of inmates, freedmen,
annexes, forests then
burdocks, nettles.
Tragic beautiful accounting.
The Better, the Verst.
The people counted not
named elsewhere:
The Oroks, the Nivkhs.
58 living residents,
40 houses.
Ideas in things.
No things but in numbers.

Americans went Wild
West. O Pioneers.
Sioux. Russians had
Wild East. Meet the Ainu.
Koreans were also
coerced to Sakhalin.
They appear in my

small grey Penguin
edition of Chekhov's *Sakhalin*
about his time in this prison
wilderness, a Russian Turner
thesis. A Second Life.

My media prison:
the island of Manhattan.
The digital interface,
my rattling train, with games
of whack-a-mole, defaced
Jewish cemeteries, hackers,
bad billionaires. Feed
after feed. Russia throwing
elections to Trump's golden tower.
Census and OSHA numbers
horribly pretty.
49,000 retail workers have
repetitive stress disability.

Chekhov in Sakhalin
briefly exchanged the T.B.
that would kill him for
the participle, innocent
men hanging in
a Siberian wilderness.
All data, all
unaccountable.

I write
the whole 19th century
was poverty porn.

Ideas in things.
No ideas but in numbers.

II.

Loud and silent islands. The *Times*
Web site blares as another
agency—mine, yours—is
dismantled. Age
of no power. Agentic layers
over non-agency,
lost gov. agencies form
an ashen impasto.

I'll take an Ativan, be
dropped off by the Via
van, in my own StreetEasy
parlor drama, a Morningside
Irina Arkadina, nettle-oil-
moisturized, my daughter's
maidenly body constricted
in her little wool uniform.
Her questions remain free.
Why do boys
have beards? Why
do women give birth?
Our doorman-keeper mutters
in Russian, "You are late."
My noise-cancelling head-
phones make
a *nouveau* quietism.

Walk to icy Hudson
River waves, rusty
steps, railroad tracks
below the bridge. Disused,
nettled, emblem of neglect,
urban taiga. As the city
grid tightens
around us.

IN BALLARD

Aquarium abuts
Hipsterium. My heart
beats fast—blame
Synthroid. That's uppers
without sin. Maybe
I'm breathless for
obelisks of lost feeling
At 6s and 7s over
my ruinous profession:
reporting used to
pay for words.

I'm near maritime condo
klatches, watering holes
that spit out old sea
dogs and walking past aging
yoginis, where breathing's
a career choice.
"Self-employed"
a synonym for still alive.
This Census is eternal.

Marriage a collective
scar tissue webbing over
extreme emotion.

"Cities like this marry
often," I say. "They
also ban drones."

You check your retweet.
"Pro-bird or
against voyeur?"
We name stuff, hope
that's proof. That's how
reporting works.
At the viewing tanks:
a ginger-tattoo-
anchored corner man,
a hot algae chick.
Sockeye-voiced,
you praise swimming
upstream, exult
in the family. I remind
that chinook splash
home and then
go DOA.
Breathe fast,
algae robots,
sprinters with gills.

As water levels
are different
for each body
of water, the lock
evens them out.
Panic is always
in a body as
well as a head.
Beside ourselves
means we are upset
but also outside our "I."

Tears a symptom
yet we are also sad.

Artisanal dives blink pink
neon, announce that
though we are far
from home we are still
somewhere.

THOUGHTS AND PRAYERS

This poem is composed of the public statements around mourning over school shootings, from political leaders and Web sites.

Designed and executed. *Us gun owners,*
Our thoughts our team's banner; our assault-
style
Thoughts and

#Prayfor

Praying impacted terrible
prayers on the scene
15 kids AR-15 pure evil
John 16:33/ horrific/ my prayers/ 1st responders

We continue to keep the victims

Kingdom of God. Columbine. Thoughts and prayers *fireside basket.* The thoughts and prayers clear mount stamp

No child, teacher: There's just no other way to describe it

Our hearts break for all the victims and families affected by today's terrible

satiation semantic civil religion common spiritual language shooting responders

The whole country stands

My heart is with Las Vegas we continue to keep the victims

My thoughts and prayers are with

$30 million in
donations. Thoughts
and prayers memes
Thoughts and Prayers: The Game,
Thoughts and Prayers tater
tots, A Thoughts and Prayers make-up tutorial with invisible cosmetics.
Fantasy red blusher: "Blood of Our Children."
Lifting up in prayer

all impacted by last night's despicable

armed teachers

relatives affected

The thoughts and prayers stamp. The thoughts and prayers handcrafted
wood card.

The thoughts and prayers angel pin.

#Prayfor

"The science" of Thoughts and Prayers.
The ostensibly mixed
research about Thoughts
and Prayers.

My heart is with Parkland. My heart is

running down the hall

shooting
our prayers

LATE CAPITALISM

A gloss and a hair mask.

Meet the shareholders?
Not at these shareholder meetings.

The best headlines have internal tension.

Band-Aids with emoji prints. I'll Venmo you. We really need concealer for our eyes. For everything.

A general practitioner available only through the special paid subscription service.

The first pot dispensary like a wine bar.

Flying the unfriendly skies.

Bush I celebrated for his decency, even by Democrats.

On C-SPAN I didn't move my face when I responded.
I did this to maintain my aura of authority.

Unpaid deductible.

Young and old play YouTube videos loud on subway cars, 11 PM.

"Where do we go when we die?": bro humor on a Stephen Colbert skit.

No wonder so many people are religious.

Just dye the roots.

My daughter holds her ears during the loud drumming of the indigenous children's play.

It may be *sensory avoidant* or it may be *childhood*.

Almond milk in the coffee drink. Lactosa nervosa.

No sulfates, no problem.

Woman's recorded voice on elevator says "lobby," the "l" obscene.

A professor of networking.

Organic daikon.

Climate-weirding: birds of the city shock us with their seasonally appropriate appearance.

The sensitivity reader made to withdraw his own book from publication due to alleged insensitivity.

Prestige TV is the new Romanticism.

The cheese plate: a hard sheep called RBG.

Is that man actually looking at me?

The billing department ultrasound bill is $736 and according to the supervisor all unpaid deductible.

I told an older man in a Dr. Zhivago–style hat and moustache (masquerade?) to lower the volume of his cellphone video on the subway.

And now another school holiday for a very minor saint: the school's founder.

Attention economy.

One woman in the South told me how she drives to the NICU so she can feel better, just going there, just holding the babies.

Wealth tax not philanthropy.

Climate weirding means no lobsters left to catch in Rhode Island.

200 pages of scandalous transcripts about rich people.

Dr. Zhivago of the subway told the man seated next to him I was obnoxious (meaning female?). He repeated himself but never addressed me directly.

The second pot dispensary like a medical spa.

On a C-SPAN show about inequality, right-wing callers tell me that immigrants steal their jobs.

Under-eye illumination cream made with diamond dust.

Some students call their pain climate anxiety.

Bush II is now a Sunday painter, depicting the very soldiers whose mutilation he ordered.

I changed subway cars to get away from Dr. Zhivago's insults.
His commentary is now called microaggressions.

How many times such things had happened to me before. I hadn't called them anything.

The indigenous children's play made me take Mother Earth seriously.

Unpaid deductible.

My organic makeup is called Vapour, a hysterical touch.

My daughter's face illuminates me.

VENTURA

Organizers may
organize closets or
workers. One
stacks the canvas
boxes of the rich.
The other
canvases people.

Gardeners blow
leaves they just
blew, plum trees
they've already
pruned. The elders
pick the fields' acrid
berries. Their sons
arrive out of season,
sleep in the street, in a dog-
house, in someone's
car. Oxnard strawberries
are plucked by hand.
No union. T Visas,
U visas. La Migra.
On the same road as
the Joads.

I eat fruit crudités
with an actor's son too
happy to get on the set
of his sicko father's

biopic. The doctor over
there is dubbed "a medical
gigolo." Not sure what
they call the selfie guy
or the California Closets
couple or the Golden Age
L.A. lawyer and his expensive
ghost. Have they accrued,
depleted, bankrupted,
hoarded? Never touching
the principal, drawing
from their trusts, split
into private educations,
creating standing?
Zero gravity:
the name of the pedicure.

Money: the phantom
limb. Have they kept
our interest?

CLINIC

1.

When we type "abortion"
autofill writes, *I am pregnant.*
I am pregnant in
Spanish. I am having
a baby and have no
insurance. I'm scared of having
a baby. What trimester am I
in. What trimester is abortion illegal?
Google says: *I need your love.*
I need an abortion.
I am pregnant can I eat shrimp?
Am I having a miscarriage?
I need help paying for abortion.
Abortion clinic violence.
Not ready to have this baby.

2.

God will punish, old ones
say in unison. They sing,
"Genocide." A man
with a Santa beard and a long gun
enters a clinic in Indiana.
In Mississippi, it's day-glo
signs, floppy hats, tiny
peachy fetus dolls.
Their lawn chairs

too near Women's Health,
their flesh sunscreen white.
Metal-detectors-
as-framing-devices.
Surveillance cameras as
glass birds.

In a place like this, in America, a long gun.

Women afraid of dying while
they are trying to find their life.

3.

On a normal day, women aged
23, 19, 41, 35.
Work at Kmart, Home Depot,
at daycares, at the hospitals
at night. Today, they learn
a new vocabulary.
Ultrasound, waiting period,
Trailways, TRAP law,
witnesses. They learn
the way euphemisms mostly tell
the truth. That the polite
word is always "discomfort."

The door clicks when it locks.
Hungry to talk. No words.

4.

She's got a cold from
her two-year-old.

The doctor talks through
the procedure. The someone
holding her hand, not
her husband.

From a Baptist town, her mother
full of God. So she lied,
got on the bus here. Drove
for three hours, borrowed
money for the hooker
motel, then the overnight
waiting period. Wondered whether
God cared or was it the care
her mother managed.
One girl was a sturdy teenager,
tall enough to play center.
Signed the parental notification
with a broken ballpoint.
Another, redheaded, the hottest
number at the Bingo Hall in
Shreveport. Grandma drank.
"What about your boyfriend?"
She answers, "He stopped
talking to me. All he wanted

was the baby."
With her own body, hurtling.

One boss wouldn't let
the woman sell car parts
if she was pregnant.
One minister called
the clinic "baby parts."

One was doing this *for
the other baby.*
The soldier said she was
doing this *so I can fight
for this country.*

5.

Plan A: the untrustworthy
Trustafarian with spotty skin.
Plan B, RU-486. Love
squashed, student leaks, summer
semester boyfriend. He brought
an apple mini pie, some orange
drink. She lay down on
her side. So many
different reproductions,
terminations. Tiered,
like experience.

6.

The ATM spits $500.
She slid inside the office
building, paid money to
a counter lady, was led into
a paneled private
room, Reagan-era
red, with fake curtains,
a bad stage set.
Silk fishtail fern,
mustard satin bedspread.
She was put to sleep

and woke up to saltines,
other posh sleepy women
in gowns, a cultic circle.
Her friend called it
"The Anaconda."
Always the code
words and then the surprise
guiltlessness.

7.

Bed rest with the mysteries. Old blood.
A mandala of succor and suffering.

Dark blood could mean anything.

It gets sloppy when you are trying to find love.

A glass of water, a small
pill. Hard candy, saltines
afterwards. Silk
flower in your hair.

8.

Poems about abortion,
poems about abortion and feelings
of sorrow. Google says: *shame or guilt;*
Remorse is Forever: Abortion Poem.
Post Abortion Stress Syndrome
Support. Poems about abortion from
a baby's point of view.

9.

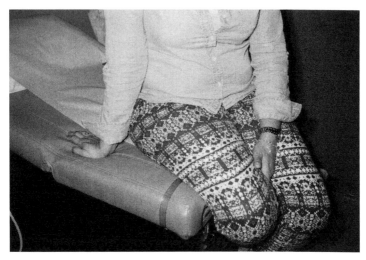

Untitled photo of Southern clinic by Jody Rogac.

Say: No shame.
We can say: The birth
spectrum. Of us:
One in four.

These choices are always field
work, freedom song, elegy,
captivity narrative.
This feeling won't forget them.
This feeling won't forget you.

II.

APOCALYPSE ANYWAY

When I believed politicians had feelings. When Gerald Ford lost the White House, on TV, crying. When George H. W. Bush was laughed at for not understanding supermarkets.

When I got into an Ivy. When I thought I was poor. When the other kids had credit cards. When they went out to restaurants where they ate chicken with prunes.

When they had their dorm rooms professionally decorated. A Roman bust stood on one girl's dresser. Her father did interiors for the Reagans.

When I discovered I wasn't poor at all.

When Donald Trump was most famous for a showgirl named Marla Maples.

When Donald and Marla were just bleached devouring creatures, just tabloid NYC.

Back when my friend had drugs in her jeans pocket, which she pulled out after her modeling jobs. When I learned women were trapped in their bodies.

When people listened to tormented music when they had sex.

When people murmured into pay phones about their mental lives, when they fucked on the phone.

The dirty snow of 1991; the blizzard of 1996 with grey ice. My black wool coat was always too thin. Hadn't learned how to keep myself warm.

When weather was literal, sometimes Modernist but not yet political.

When female writers made their names denying other women's suffering.

When I couldn't pay my rent.

When Bill Clinton was President and read a lot but also made poor people pick up garbage by the side of highways.

When a pundit said *alpha men, earth tones.*

When I started in the homage business. When I started in the lament business.

When my favorite feeling was dirty nostalgia.

When I read *Dispatches* in a public park while my boyfriend worked at the State Department.

Is is.

When the next boyfriend bought Prada shoes.

When I wore an A-line dress in a 1930s green that I bought near my therapist's office, my blanched skinny legs, all underbelly.

When I still had a therapist because I was young and had no money— such sliding scale—and she thought my misery had promise.

When I always wore chokers, as if symbolizing that I could withstand male aggression.

When suddenly coffee was expensive. When people started moving to Seattle. When they started moving to Portland. Then going off the grid.

When Y2K was scary. When Y2K was a joke. When architects constructed Y2K-themed buildings.

When frosty palettes implied a future present.

When I woke up, biked downtown, talked to everyone.

When the smell: the industrial products, the cooked brown sugar, the rubber, the bodies.

When after September 11th, burning buildings were collateral for wars without ends.

When I biked at night with no backlights because it was apocalypse anyway.

When Arianna Huffington ran for governor of California against the child actor Gary Coleman. The late Coleman preferred his toy trains, however, to the campaign trail.

When elections went tabloid but we hadn't realized yet what that would mean.

When men who haunted women were still called "cads."

When people stopped talking on the phone.

When people started talking about TV shows rather than gossiping. When people didn't talk much at all.

When loving books became a vulnerability. When writing them turned into a liability.

When people started taking Prozac. When people started taking Ambien.

When I stopped believing in student debt.

When I realized time was killing us.

The protest sign "We Shall Over Comb."

When other people became my religion.

When I didn't think of anyone else.

When all I thought about was other people.

PASS

"Pass over.
Pass over.
Pass.
Pass.
Pass."

Gertrude Stein & Jerome
Rothenberg both played
word games that split
Passover in half.
Rothenberg writes
"pass" in upper
case and "jewish" in lower
case, as if to both disown
and "casual" these words.
Their matching poems
are an entry into writing
a "jewish poem"
as Rothenberg says.
Neither imagined
appropriation rotted out
the original. Their version
of Passover: symbolic,
like the holiday.
Blood on the doors of the first
born. Kosher cough syrup
for holiday wine,
flat bread standing in
for slavery, salty

water for tears, walnuts
in a blender for shelter.
Shankbone approx.-ed by
a cardboard bone, when
I was a vegan.

Pass over.

Because language and the physical
world don't correspond &
words don't express
full internal selves,
or space or time.

Pass over.

Life mostly symbols, analogies that tie
us to each other, shadows
on the cave, the flickering
correspondences,
truer as we age,
an idea of the world in our head
composed of papier-mâché
layers of different times,
or selves. No real world
can resemble our inner
mentality without huge gaps.

Armand Schwerner, another avant-
garde Jewish poet, advised
me at 20 to stay vanguard.
I was a late New York
School Red Diaper

Moppet. Half
his tongue was removed
after cancer, cancelation
of his song.
He is not so
remembered and
not so celebrated
now as perhaps
he should be. I will recall
and celebrate him,
like bitter herbs or salt
water for tears. He wrote:
"go into all the places you're frightened of
and forget why you came, like the dead
what should I look for?"
The experimental Jewish
poets are funny and morbid.
"...who is my friend? a little stone,
a lot of dirt, a terrible headache."

Passover.

We are boxes with no bottoms,
tops. Within these cardboard cubes
we float downwards,
sliding through memories,
without fundament,
as if fungible.

We love each other
still though so tired. Wish
we knew the Hebrew songs,

so we might pass
and also Passover
Up to our necks
in gluten-free bread-
crumbs; apartment
searches; that nasty red
at Henry's resto. Foreign
and constricted
in the temples around us.
So ersatz that the yoga
prayer is more familiar,
or moving. It's all
confusing, in a holy tongue
we do not know but
where others find
warming peace.

Pass over.
Stein's poem
about Passover
became Rothenberg's
when he adds
the snicker "pass water."
Both remind me that Jews
might be America's
experimentalists. Also
that Judaism is not always
experimental enough.
Pass over.

Pass over.

PRE-NATAL

Summer bike rides at night,
no backlights. A citrine
knotted on a black ribbon.
Something faster.
Phosphorescent line,
broken asphalt. Bianchi
bike bumped. Precious,
phony, fun. Peddling
out of the dark.
All the things
adults do alone.

Never have kids, said Alysia,
my friend and name-
double, in her house's mud
room, New England,
eating cornichons
like she always served.
Her baby screaming
upstairs tore off his sheets.

I left her house, unlocked
my bike, with no thought
of anyone. My tight
black jeans. Passed the Star
Market then the bar
as lumpen poured out
then the anarcho silk-
screen-ers as they alighted

on the street. Late youth
meant no permanent
marks or maybe none
by my own hand. Nights
still possible, sharp,
almost inhalable.
Road torn
up and underlit
yet still intact.

COTERIE

I.

We analyze the dead
to protect us from
their aggressions.
"He just ran
out of road."
"Life is so short: he could
have waited."
"He was
so self-involved."
Do we imagine we
were closer, or not
as close?

Solidarity a brand
now squeezed by
these coastal cities.
Soon a coterie poem
like this will no
longer occur
to anyone.

II.

With your middle-
aged roommate, rent-
controlled, sometimes no
money, your films

composed on a bench,
in your mind, on
the median. Your city
now turning on
your kind: aging,
melancholic, itinerant,
eyes shiny, listening to near-
strangers cry, nodding to
the semi-tragic story
of someone's mother.
Pretty, plaid
shirt, hair in your
ears, grasping
my wrist, wanting
to kiss, who, me, a woman,
the indeterminate sexed.
Entranceways or sub-
way doors, closing.
What was left in
your account? Your
refrains: you had a new
idea, you needed funds.

You tied a string or a tie
or a belt. I never knew which.
Tied to a fixed object. Fought
the instinct to fight.

III.

Our adults instructed us:
Follow your dreams;
Do what you love.

Post-counter-
culture assent.
I'm sliding you into my neo-
Marxism, says R,
I know you
belong there, though,
once a middle-class
kid pinched by the rich
and then the new
achievers, in the medication-
blue-walled school. Our
hacky-sack expressivities,
our dime-bag pleasures,
and infinite numbers.
Our classes teaching us
our given radii.
Soon we'd be
vectored by status,
a hard-edged drafting
tool, ruling
out communality.

IV.

A stranger at midnight Face-
Times me from L.A. to talk,
your death already a text.
She was in a 90s R&B
band. Former lover/confidante? Like the other
foxy women
with fine skin and early
credits on IMDB.
Were you especially sad?

Going to the daily group
therapy, accepting your
mental states, no
longer eating bread,
planning to get married,
listening carefully, with
your strange laugh,
sucking on those
cannabis lollipops.

Could I have taken
better care? Should I have
gone to your place, eaten
the edibles from L.A.
Do I pretend we were
closer than we
were. Do I also pretend
that we were not.

AGAINST AMNESIA

After the Peter Hujar show "The Speed of Life" at the Morgan Library, May 2018.

Granite waves, geese,
half-rotten meals, half-rotten
boys. Between death and life.
(True of every-
one.) In 1983
the mask and its slippage
were one: grave
silken prints, silver
gelatin. He mastered
harder minds and men,
kept feline profligates
in line.

The Hujar show
at the Morgan:
a Leica is an anti-
amnesiac tool.
Pale, etched young
men—dancers, trade—
made to the measure
of others' desire.
Sitters' NYC
pidgin names:
Ethyl, Lavinia Co-op.

"Christopher Street Pier #2 (Crossed Legs)" by Peter Hujar.

Sexy horses, languorous
freaks, warmly lurid
bedsheets show us how
we might have lived.
Avedon and Arbus are
chintzy voyeurs compared
to his unfolded intensity,
his sitters' value neither
reduced nor enlarged.
He—and they—
suspended between
presence and disappearance,
the real undead.
Sarah Jenkins, nude, in a head
brace worn like a demented
halo. Creatures
of Downtown: near my
Montessori-by-Badlands.
1970s of the mind,
of freedom, where transgod-
mothers loomed. Later,
some turned to ash
or maybe afterlife
or worse, reality
shows on Bravo.
Hujar's places dissolve
also. World Trade Center
West Street piers
The Village Voice.
Arising from these scenes
he is now sealed into them as

a grey cold seam of lament
runs down each picture.
Tainted saint of the abused
he looked into the sitters'
eyes then out of them,
all at once.

OUTRAGEOUS

In the devouring eighties, Roxy roller-skating, I dreamed I'd grow to be a Romantic Hudson St. queen, merely teen.

One day I became Andre the Giant, the next stenciled Revs, reading paperback poetry under the table in the library.

Sex with a boy kimono-clad might involve ropes and a radiator.

The Story of the Eye at 16 had its costs.

Best friend E. didn't wash and spoke early Greek, "got lost" with strangers before an unplanned son. Kipped in my bed in a retro silk housedress.

Grown men ranted.

I survived on what. The grimy stanzas from the used bookstore on Charles, walking night miles in those thin Chinese slippers till my feet hurt more than fear of home.

Smoking because I/she/we were burning.

The nightlife: outrageous but without today's outrage. Women on swings like *Wings of Desire*. I could be them? In my vintage red bandleader shirt, with the ogee of gold sequins.

One day, I spied a local celeb literally buying milk in a bodega, His Majesty Quentin Crisp.

He was not like the men who stained women's arms newsprint shades, or the men covered in greasy newsprint.

Crisp's violet attire: non-violence itself.

His plumed hat.

What happened next: the *Sex and the City* props, the fat beats from corporate hip-hop.

My home memories pour back into myself, unbidden. They return now, after thirty years, as nightmares or dreams, some of pixie boys, semi-dressed.

Benzo sleep, heavy on the bass, some more terrors or the most adrenal dreams.

MS. THINGS

"Thing" written on
my arm, smoky
eyeliner. As girls-to-women
we were always
in costume. The bigger
girl went as "Object."
Ms. Things.

Our pre-war apts. from the alt
weekly. Strange roommates
prayed at household altars,
or were narcoleptics.
We hopped, kept
our gamine-faces on
while the boys had their *arcs*,
looping from the mail
rooms to the assistant-
ships, clambering up
the ruddy mastheads.
Meanwhile we called
careers "careens."
Lizard editors left messages
on our machines.
Really, I've got to
fuck you.
We were the distaff
with no extra room.
That is no
fantasy space.

Some boys beat off on
the unwilling, traded favors.
Their *alte kaker*
mentors in on it (maybe)
too. They then retired
or, as they say, were
downsized. In our diction,
literary executions replaced
literary executors.
To some I whisper
Fuck you.

I am not a thing now
but still a woman
so that makes me a
not-thing.

We can write the word
on our arms now,
not turning on
anyone. This is
the prize time
affords us.

FEVER

Baby temp. 104
we war over
ibuprofen as if
you're a Christian
Scientist. I think I may
rise. Our baby, our kitten.
She's a feeding thing.
When she was six
months old, I tried
to go for a year
but she had five
teeth by month four so
landed me in that store
The Upper Breast
Side, its owner asking
"Who's lactating
on the floor?"
Our house got decor
fatigue. Her body hurt
me like the world.

Where was the formula?
I searched in secret,
the supplementary supplement.

Her fever high now,
we cab to the ER, where other
tots wear masks to
breathe, look like clear

baby elephants. I remember
why kids are breathless:
leaders' lies; growing
up near dumps or highways.
Ours will be
mended. Standing near
the ward's zebra mural,
our baby smiles sickly,
turning her lantern
face to me.

Kindly doctors with urine
cups find out what's wrong
and bills cascade, candy-
pink syrup released by
dropper in her mouth
as if holy. When baby finally
sleeps, we read and maybe
attack each other.

A breast milk Christ,
a leaking action
painting, the American mother:
a Prisoner's other
Dilemma. Lower
the temperature to
stop the screaming.

ALPHABETICAL AMERICA

A is for the "anti's" closing clinics in Alabama

B for birthdays of bedazzling, bank holidays of bruxing

C for constant crisis

D for damaged D lines, for a daguerreotype app

E is for energy, the thing that the crystal people think will save us

F for framing devices and the frisson over the framers

G for gonzo journalists working gig jobs

H is for hat tips, for the hate-filled, for the hapless heteros, for hamantaschen

I is for the ICE high schools

J is for the jonquil-scented personal journey

K is for kale eaters: micro politics equal micro greens

L is for loser—i.e., what the president calls people

M is for militias moving from the edge to the center

N is for the neurotics negging each other

O: the black olive eyes, the *oh* that we come from & return to

P is for payday lenders

Q is for quasi-queer

R is for rampant and sometimes random resistance

S is for a spa so-and-so, that Sister in the sun

T is for the TMJ disorder tracking the tender-hearted

U: the ushering out of Frank Underwood

V: the violet vendettas of the victimized

W: the open-carry West

X is a president's x-cised x-rated actresses, xciting and hopefully xiting

Y: the yard in NIMBY

Z is for zeroes belonging to the richest, to nothingness, to binary

MAMMO

My smiling blonde
technician, a Chernobyl
escapee, remembers nuclear
rain, "The sun, the drops
at once." May Day
'86, she and her young son
parading with marching
bands in toxic winds.
"We should
have stayed inside."

She now controls the 3-D
apparatus, the areola-
squeezers, the Vegas-gone-
medical, outpatient spa
pasties. Adele muzak—
literally, that's 1,000 tiny
violins playing. Are we saved
by pink robes;
these artful strobes?
Screening-as-meaning.
Who knows?

No need for that novel
where a man becomes
boob (Philip Roth).
Women are always
breasts and forced
yet clever surrealists.

We are examined,
neglected, or over-
scrutinized,
covered in hot ejaculate
of sonogram or
caught in vises.
Blushing. Dense. Well-
maintained.

Her current job in
radiation is ironic,
the technician knows.
She says, "Distrust
leaders everywhere.
Still, it's better here. For
example, the rain."

III.

MRI

The magnetic life-
sized machine sounds
mistakes. The worst
one: allowing
youth to end.

They give you a checklist
of American destruction.
Does your body
have shrapnel? Tattoos
meant to change
your life? A nose
pierce? The false
hip. The metal
knee: arrows.
Pinned elbows:
sportif wands.
The breast implant meant
to make him
love you. Or,
yes, god knows, the penile.

Within the imaging
capsule, the sound
of robots, of iron
chains whining loose,
ferries in black water
thumping their metal
crossings, a forgotten

nightclub, a subway's
halting sparks,
stranger music.

They'll check for metal,
stone, mass, rip, tear.
If your ring is real, it won't
hurt. If it aches,
you'll know
how little he spent
to make you his.

The machine
knows: we're all
Saint Sebastian.

THE HARASSER'S APOLOGY

I always felt I was
pursuing shared feelings

I am suffering
the same treatment

A wake-
up call

I wish I had
reacted to their
admiration of me

conquer my demons

I wielded that power

I came of age
when all the rules

Different script

I was mistaken

I've brought anguish
and hardship

As a man

This story has
encouraged me
to address

other things.

a good example to them

Wake up

I believe tampering
has occurred.

I am sorry for the feelings
he describes having carried

I moved on
her like
a bitch.

I so respect all
women.

ENCLAVE

Fear not ruling more than
            not being.

The armor: white
shirts, black cloches, grey
clogs. Hidden
            but valuable
            logos as tribal seals.

At the table the chef narrates how
            each animal,
            each vegetable
            died.

Happiness, the province
            of the rich.

Advanced degree
            women. Money
            guys.

In the enclave mothers
renovate, and paint
is a smart
matte choice.
            Murmuring Owl Grey,
            Supreme White, Worsted,
            Dead Flat, Estate
            Eggshell, Powder White.

Invitation to the winter
benefit sent to the five-year-old,
tickets start at three hundred.

The gamekeeper, the contractor, the paint consultant.

Older heiresses there
like to be called BABY.
The women want to have
sex with their houses.
        Their bracelets' leather
        implies falsely that
        they will submit.

House paint subs for sex
here. One lady's color
is Inchrya. A vibrating
blue. There are wild
berry souvenirs drying
in clay bowls.

You are not in the right
        place when you are
        near power. You are not in
        the right place yet
        always somehow there.

Happiness, an enclave.

WEDDING POEM

January 2017

This bright day broke a dark election for us, those who combine lustration with lust.

Hypervigilant, we look awry at alpine landscapes, palmy beaches, seals and their harbors.

We know each place, each further election, might bring terror or a need for protection.

We are dyslexic to convention. We read the world picture in reverse. Athens, Tel Aviv, Paris.

Forgiveness also needs protection.

Like the sea lions, we are political animals.

Begone Brexit loca-bores and rich-mouthing TEDs.

We clink glasses. "Here's to Spanish as a first language," "Here's to snowy prole origins." "Here's to acquired vices—Blue State merlot, exoteric essays, and peep-toe shoes."

Our faith—that tragedy can be corralled, that we might become a safe haven in the regime. That marriage is a third citizenship.

Forgiveness always needs protection.

23ANDME

Bloody archive whose attendant
        story lines are twisted,
like braided helixes. Its tests revealed
        a woman's dad was a Civil
Rights noble not that hateful
        local schlub, another the issue
of an icy Goy. My dear R. found her ogre
        grandpa had three kids
        all on the D.L.: Lothario, donor, or still
not sure? A genetic memory play, or born-agains
        with private science as Revelation.
No wonder the company's founder was married to Google's.
        Another entity that finds almost everything
yet never what we need (the Unseen). No, really.
        Help me! Nothing can reorder flesh tho
that was made half a century ago
        Iberian, Neanderthal, broadly sub-Saharan, poetically
unassigned. Meet your genes, 23andMe
        or perhaps Ancestry LLC.
But surely you have already met yourself.

CANCEL THIS

On Twitter today they say: cancel this. Cancel that. Cancel the Second Wave Feminists. Cancel Ancient Sumer, the Euphrates, the well-oiled feet of Telemachus.

The platform then cries, "Apologize, apologize."

How to not be called out? On Twitter, YouTube, the 'Gram: make makeup tutorials; adopt a single name; worry strictly about your algorithm; order food good enough to look at
but not to eat.

Cancel civilization.

Or maybe not.

Cancel canceling the Greeks.

Listen to Athena. Girl, your symbolic mothers still circle round the islands, hopefully with their lovers, while the fathers are with Circe and Co. Women's minds are wild. Protect their honor. It is yours as well.

ALMA MATER

On the 10:03 morning train, on my way to teach in Providence, I realize that returning to old schools a regret machine, as is middle age itself.

Characters return to their alma maters in movies.

Like *Brad's Status*, a Ben Stiller film that nobody saw. Brad compares himself to the glossy and rich guys in his class: one frolics on a beach with two young girlfriends. He trails his polished son around his alma mater, an Ivy. Brad suffers a panic attack.

Arriving at the city of my old college to teach each week, I walk past Providence's saltbox houses, painted their stern, elegant colors, on my way to my short-lived office.

I stop for the chicory salad from a farm-to-table restaurant called something like The Salted Slate because of what I have read of Sylvia Plath's year teaching literature at her alma mater Smith College. In her letters about that miserable time she writes of serving chicory salad to undesired dinner guests. I am hoping my salad will taste like the one she made for dining companions she despised.

In Providence, one is always walking down or up a hill. I do so and think of Plath, of her skipping Northampton for Boston and psychoanalysis. I too could have gone back in time in a different way, like analysis, rather than returning to my alma mater this semester.

Brad's Status is a movie about middle-aged longing that is labeled a comedy. It is anything but.

The night train takes me back home. I squint to make out the outline of New England.

Plath wrote of her loneliness and how she made herself have dinner with other Northamptonites four times a week. She described them hatefully, depicting professors' "dowdy seat-spread wives," and felt alien on campus as an instructor, "apart, aware of apartness & a strange oddity."

The word "relive" inverts to the word "revile."

The rough coastline is glowing, as it is during the day.

Of the poets I knew in the 1990s, the late Reginald Shepherd could be said to be the most classical, lyrical and even Plath-like. I befriended him when I was still a teenager in Providence. Unlike Plath, he was born poor. In a poem of his I remember: "Mineral seams just under the skin."

In her misery at Smith in 1957, she mastered what she called "domesticalia" in part by baking mother's sponge cake. For Plath and other women of that era, cooking and entertaining were seemingly an *anti-poetry*. No permission for breaks.

In *Brad's Status*, Brad is "wanting" in every sense. He asks why what happened happened, and what has the time meant.

I buy my morning Acela train ticket, visualizing an express train as a metal bough.

When I say Acela, it sounds like the Acacia, the flower of Romanticism.

I only did what I could, placing other people's words & bodies in front of any wounds.

I am on the 10:03 AM to Providence.

THE CLOUD

From the words of former FBI director James Comey.

And then the nature
of the person

To lift the cloud

Criminal in nature

Turning

Grandfather clock

A whole lot of personal pain

Lifting the cloud

Being somebody who loves
this country

These were lies

The nature of its work

As a cloud

Grandfather clock

Lie about the nature
meant by the cloud

Turning over rocks

Grandfather clock

The cloud

That's wonderful and painful
big messy wonderful country

SUMMER HAVEN

Power tans itself, roasts
another rack of bream.

At the summer party
he's toasted for
not destroying his
own home.

The oyster shucker
is the truest philanthropist.

"There are no real
people left here," said
the engineer.

I want in. I want
in. "Imagine
meeting you at
the beach!"
The only note-
book to be
found, of cream–
colored handmade
paper. Deface such
pages with my pen?
Vetiver and lemon–
grass blend.
"House poor."

Boarding school visible
in a woman's island
tan, her Sanskrit tattoo.
Want, want, in.

Affordable housing for
the fisherman and his
wife? Maybe next year.

My family name
is no name, I am a house-
guest in adulthood.

The son's rock fest:
his final prep
school extra-curric.
The wampum
pendants. The handmade
perfume oils with pepper
notes. Sword-
fish, a 12-dollar hybrid
peach. 100 percent
cotton cover-ups hide
mortal bums.

We can't afford
to own adulthood.

All attended
same school.
Sedate comforted

plover protected
but not from plunder

started with the Indians.

Crème fraîche from
happy cows;
lavender hand-
harvested. Colostrum-
like caramel.
The best children's
book collection.
Here lake
combines with sea.

Are we house-
guests in adulthood?

Buoyed by our netting,
our private instruction,
nettled and consoled
by our origins.

Everything can go
on the grill.

Notes

Sakhalin This poem derives from my reading an expurgated version of Anton Chekhov's *Sakhalin Island* during the time following Donald Trump's 2016 presidential win. It is titled *A Journey to the End of the Russian Empire*, comprised of Chekhov's letters reporting his travels in 1890 to the penal island of Sakhalin. He crossed Siberia by train, then traveled on a steamer. In Sakhalin, he conducted a census of remote settlements. He was struck by how prisoners and exiles were free to move about in their desolate Elba, but so degraded by isolation, among other hardships, that they were still imprisoned.

Thoughts and Prayers This poem is composed of the public language around mourning over school shootings in the U.S. or from political leaders and Web sites. I also sifted through the language that politicians of both parties tweet, what kids themselves said about mass shootings, and the words companies use in fabricating souvenirs that commodify mass killings.

Clinic This poem is a filtered version of interviews with more than two dozen women I spoke with at abortion clinics, counseling service offices, and pregnancy centers in Mississippi, Indiana, and New York, and short films and features on this topic that I have worked on "The Last Clinic," "Reconception," and "Jackson." I think of the poem as a meta-text around this reporting.

Pass This poem was written on the occasion of a Passover seder in 2016. My friend Julie Lasky asked all the guests to present a holiday-themed piece of writing, song or art.

The Harasser's Apology In this poem, I take verbatim statements of famous men who have (yes, allegedly) sexually harassed, assaulted, or raped women (or, in one case, other men). These include written statements and transcripts from Harvey Weinstein, Louis C.K., Roy Moore, Kevin Spacey, Charlie Rose, and Donald Trump.

Alphabetical America I wrote this poem in 2018, after Anne Carson's "L.A." in *Float*. The "gonzo journalists working gig jobs" are people I have both hired and written about as a nonfiction writer and a nonprofit executive director. "I is for the ICE high schools" refers to a documentary that my nonprofit Economic Hardship Reporting Project has supported.

Wedding Poem This poem was composed for and read on the occasion of the marriage of two friends who are law professors.

The Cloud This is former FBI director James Comey's Senate Intelligence Committee testimony reconfigured as a free-form verse. I found the transcript strangely poetic. For instance, Comey's constant references to the grandfather clock were practically Poe-esque. Some have speculated Comey included these multiple mentions for legal reasons, to prove that he was actually in the room with President Trump. The clock, by the way, is a Seymour tall case, 8 feet 10 inches, and is known commonly as the Oval Office grandfather clock.

Acknowledgments

As the great poet George Oppen wrote, "We have chosen the meaning./ Of being numerous." A multitude of remarkable colleagues and friends have assisted in the making of this volume. The first is my beloved agent, Jill Grinberg, and the helpful and literate women who work with her, Denise Page and Sophia Seidner. Then there is the clever and committed editorial support of Colin Robinson and Emma Ingrisani at OR Books and the elegant efforts of OR cover designer Antara Ghosh. I also must thank my inspired and dear pal Astra Taylor for helping to make this collection into an OR reality.

I also must offer appreciation to the artist Jack Pierson, whose luminous photo graces the cover, and to Jim Lewis for his help in midwifing. The irreplaceable dEEN modino did incredible cover mock-ups at a rapid clip. Rachel Urkowitz also offered her astute aesthetic consultations.

I also owe multiple, marvelous friend-editors praise for their close reading of this text and their careful notes. Mark Bibbins was a grammar whiz. Katy Lederer's strong direction helped make this a book in the first place. Camille Guthrie, Celina Su, Anne Kornhauser, and Ann Peters offered excellent advice on everything from line breaks to poem inclusion to copyediting. Thank you Laura Strausfeld for encouraging me to give this book a visual component. Thanks also to Laura Raicovich, Chris Nealon, Hanya Yanagihara, Michael Coffey, Sarah Safer, and Maia Szalavitz for your assistance and thoughts.

I am in debt to the great Mary Gaitskill, Wayne Koestenbaum, Eileen Myles, Barbara Ehrenreich and Karen Bender. Thanks also Rachael Allen, Devorah Baum, and David Wallis. I so appreciate the generosity of Jody Rogac and Hedi Sorger and Stephen Koch at the Peter Hujar Archive for the photos within the book's pages.

Susan Minot is in a category of her own for her copious and superb edits.

And finally, as always, my love and gratitude go to Peter Maass and Cleo Quart Maass, without whom there would be no poetry.

© Ash Fox

Alissa Quart is a poet and a nonfiction writer. She is the executive director of the Economic Hardship Reporting Project. Quart's first poetry book is *Monetized* (Miami University Press, 2015). Her poems have appeared in *Granta*, the *London Review of Books*, *The Nation*, NPR, *Fence*, *Columbia Journalism Review*, *The Offing*, and the *Poetry Society of America*, among others.

She writes regularly for *The Guardian*, *The New York Times*, and many other publications. Her four nonfiction books are *Squeezed: Why Our Families Can't Afford America* (Ecco/HarperCollins), *Republic of Outsiders* (New Press), *Hothouse Kids* (Penguin Press), and *Branded* (Basic Books). Quart has taught journalism most recently at Brown University and Columbia University's Graduate School of Journalism. Quart is Columbia Journalism School's 2018 Alumna Award recipient, was a 2010 Nieman fellow at Harvard University, and in 2018 received an Emmy award for executive producing the Best Documentary, Social Issue, "Jackson."